COME & ADORE HIM

A CHRISTMAS MUSICAL FOR SENIOR ADULT CHOIR

Created by Dave Clark

Arranged and Orchestrated by Steve W. Mauldin

lillenas.com

Contents

Come and Adore Him

with

Angels, from the Realms of Glory

Words and Music by
REBECCA PECK
Arr. by Steve W. Mauldin

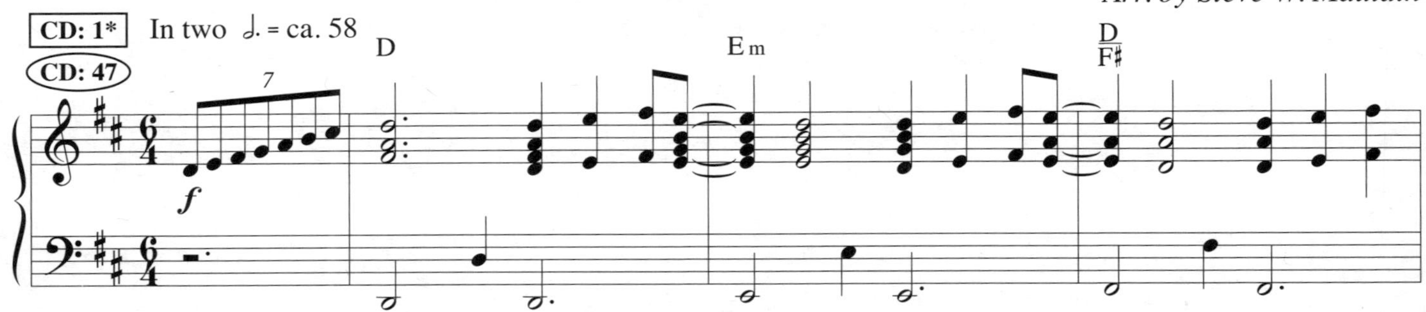

*CD POINTS: Split-channel, CD:1-46; Stereo Trax, CD:47-92

11
Him, Wor-ship the Lord of lords; Come in-to His
E♭/G
A♭M7
B♭
E♭
14
pres-ence, Glo-ry and rev-'rence, Be to His name ev-er-more.
Fm7
E♭/G
A♭M7
B♭
17
God Him-self, here to dwell a-mong men;
G/B
Cm
F/A
B♭
A♭2

CD: 2
CD: 48
20
Come, come and a - dore
A♭2
Fm7/4
A♭/G
A♭M7
B♭sus
B♭
23
Him.
Come, come and a-dore
E♭
E♭/B♭
C sus
C
F
26
Him, Fall - ing be-fore Him, Wor-ship the Lord of lords;
Gm7
F/A
B♭M7
C

29
Come in - to His pres - ence, Glo - ry and rev - 'rence, Be to His
F
Gm7
F/A
32
name ev - er - more. God Him - self, here to dwell a - mong
B♭M7
C
A/C♯
Dm
G/B
C
35
men; Come, come and a -
B♭2
Gm7/4
B♭/A
B♭M7

*Words by JAMES MONTGOMERY; Music by HENRY T. SMART. Arr.

49
mel.
Ye who sang cre - a - tion's sto - ry, Now pro-claim Mes - si - ah's birth.
G
B
D♯
Em
B
F♯
Em
G
D
A
A7
D
53
CD: 4
CD: 50
Come and wor - ship. Come and wor - ship. Wor - ship Christ, the
D
D
C
B
B
D♯
Em
Am
G
B
Am
C
C
E
56
new - born King. Shep - herds, in the field a - bid - ing, Watch - ing o'er your
Dsus
D
G
G
C
G
G

flocks by night, God with man is now re-sid-ing; Yon-der shines the mel. In-fant Light.
Come and wor-ship. Come and wor-ship. Wor-ship Christ, the new-born King.
Come and wor-ship. Come and wor-ship.
CD: 5
CD: 51

Segue to "What Child Is This?"

*NARRATOR: In the Word of God it is written that an angel of the Lord appeared unto Mary and spoke these words, "Do not be afraid, Mary. You have found favor with God. You will be with child and give birth to a son, and you are to give him the name Jesus. He will be great and will be called the Son of the Most High. The Lord God will give him the throne of his father David, and he will reign over the house of Jacob forever; his kingdom will never end."

What Child Is This?

WILLIAM C. DIX

Traditional English Melody
Arr. by Steve W. Mauldin

17
sleep - ing? Whom an - gels greet with
A7
Dm
C/E
F
21
CD: 7
CD: 53
an - thems sweet, While shep - herds watch are
C
Am
Dm
A7
25
CHOIR div.
mf
keep - ing?
This, this is
Dm
F
Dm

29
Christ, the King, Whom shep - herds guard and
Em
Am
B♭M7
Gm
33
an - gels sing. Haste, haste to
A
F
Dm
37
bring Him laud, The Babe, the Son of
Em
Am
Dm
Am
C
B♭
A7

CD: 8
CD: 54
Mar - y.
Dsus
Dm
B♭M7 Am7 Gm7
A A7
MEN unis.
(Optional Solo)
mf
So bring Him in - cense,
Dsus
Dm
CD: 9
CD: 55
gold, and myrrh; Come, peas - ant, king to
C
B♭

53
Add LADIES
mf
King of kings sal -
own Him. The King of kings sal -
A 7
D m
C
E
F
57
mel.
mel.
va - tion brings; Let lov - ing hearts en -
va - tion brings;
C
A m
D m
A 7
61
f
throne Him. This,
f
D m
6
F
f

64
this is Christ, the King, Whom shep - herds
Dm
Em
Am
B♭M7
68
guard and an - gels sing.
Haste,
Gm
A
F
72
dim. poco a poco
haste to bring Him laud, The Babe, the
dim. poco a poco
Dm
Em
Am
Am/C
Dm
Am/C
B♭
dim. poco a poco

76

rit. mp slower

Son of Mar - y. The Babe, the

A7 Dsus Dm B♭M7 Am7 Gm7

rit. mp slower

80

rit.

Son of Mar - y.

A7 Dsus

rit.

8va

(Without music)

NARRATOR: One night while shepherds were in the field watching their flock, an angel of the Lord suddenly appeared saying: "Do not be afraid. I bring you good news *(music begins)* of great joy that will be for all people. Today in the town of David a Savior has been born to you; he is Christ the Lord." *(Luke 2:10-11)*

It's Still Good News

Words and Music by
DAVE CLARK and
BEV HERREMA
Arr. by Steve W. Mauldin

11
watch - ing their flocks by night; As the
E♭
B♭
CD: 11
CD: 57
13
an - gel ap - peared God's glo - ry was re - vealed, as the
B♭
15
LADIES unis.
mf
But the
heav - ens were filled with light.
C7
F7

17
CD: 12
CD: 58
an - gel said, "Don't be a - fraid, for Christ is born to
E♭
D 7
G m
20
you to - day." It's still good news,
Add MEN mf It's still
C 7sus
C 7
N.C.
B♭6
B♭
23
it's still great joy;
good news, it's still great joy; What
B♭
G 9
G 7

26

an-gels said to shep-herd men was more than just a sto-ry

E♭ B♭/D C7

29

way back when; It's still good news, It's still

E♭M7/F E♭6/F N.C. B♭6 B♭

32

it's still great joy;
good news, it's still great joy;

B♭ G9 G7

35
God sent His Son, Christ has come, and it's
E♭
C7
D7
Gm
CD: 13
CD: 59
37
still good news to - day.
C7
F7sus
F7
B♭2
B♭
40
The good news is that no
MEN unis. mf
Gm2
Gm
B♭

43
mat - ter where we are the Light of the world still shines;
B♭
E♭
45
CD: 14
CD: 60
And it's call - ing to us to come in from the dark and
B♭
48
Add LADIES div.
mf
leave our fears be - hind.
For Christ has come to
C7
F7
E♭

CD: 15
CD: 61
51 
seek and to save and e - ven now the Sav - ior waits.
D7
Gm
C7sus
54
f
It's still good news, it's still
f
It's still good news,
C7
N.C.
f
B♭6
B♭
57
great joy;
it's still great joy;
What an-gels said to
G9
G7
E♭

60

shep - herd men was more than just a sto - ry

B♭ C7

62

way back when;

It's still good news,

It's still

E♭M7/F E♭6/F N.C. B♭6 B♭

65

it's still great joy;

good news, it's still great joy;

B♭ G9 G7

68
God sent His Son, Christ has come, and it's still good news to-day.
E♭
C7
D7
Gm
C7
F7sus
F7
CD: 16
CD: 62
71
God sent His Son,
B♭2
E♭
C7
74
Christ has come, and it's still good news to-day.
D7
Gm
C7
F7sus
F7
B♭

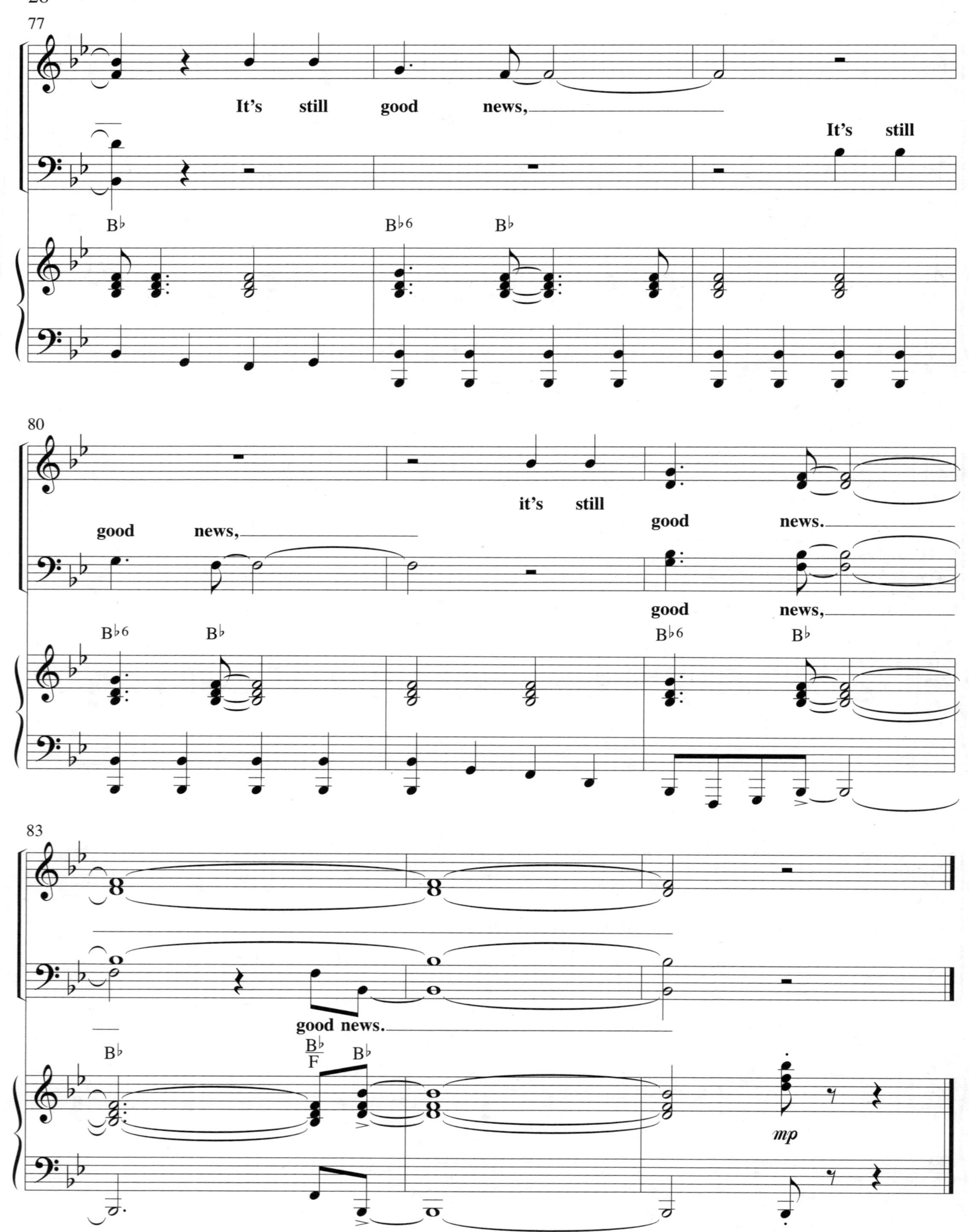
77
It's still good news,
It's still
B♭
B♭6
B♭
80
good news,
it's still
good news.
good news,
B♭6
B♭
B♭6
B♭
83
good news.
B♭
B♭/F
B♭
mp

The Birthday of a King

with
Infant Holy, Infant Lowly

Words and Music by
WILLIAM H. NEIDLINGER
Arr. by Steve W. Mauldin

CD: 18
CD: 64
sky was bright with a ho - ly light o'er the place where Je - sus
Em G/D G/B A A/G D/F♯ G D/A G/A A7
lay.
mf
Al - le - lu - ia! O how the an - gels sang! Al - le -
Add MEN unis. mf
Al - le -
Dsus D C/D Fm/D D7 G D/F♯
mf
lu - ia!
lu, Al - le - lu - ia! How it rang! And the sky was bright with a
lu - ia!
Em A7 D Am/C B B/D♯ Em Em/C♯
2/4

24
ho - ly light; 'Twas the birth - day of a
G/D D#°7 Em E♭7 G/D D7
27
Al - le -
King. Al - le - lu - ia! O how the an - gels sang! Al - le -
Al - le -
G C/D Fm/D D7 G D/F#
30
lu - ia!
lu, Al - le - lu - ia! How it rang! And the sky was bright with a
lu - ia!
Em A7 D Am/C B B/D# Em Em/C#

*NOTE: Ladies can get their pitches from the Men's notes.

42
sky was bright with a ho - ly light; 'Twas the
B
B/D♯
Em
Em/C♯
G/D
D♯°7
Em7
E♭7
45
birth - day, 'Twas the birth - day
mp
G/D
Em7
E♭7
G/D
48
rit.
of a King.
CM7/D
D7
G
N.C.

*Words and Music Polish Carol.

62
Babe, is Lord of all. Swift are wing - ing an - gels
F/A Gm/B♭ F/C C7 F F/A B♭2 B♭ Gm
65
sing - ing, no - els ring - ing, tid - ings bring - ing: Christ, the
C2 C Am Dm2 Dm B♭/D C2/E C/E C7 C7/B♭
CD: 21
CD: 67
68
Babe, is Lord of all! Christ, the Babe, is Lord of
F/A Gm/B♭ F/C C♯°7 Dm Am/C C7/B♭ F/A Gm/B♭ F/C C7

71
all!
Flocks were sleep - ing; shep - herds
F
N.C.
F
C/F
F
74
keep - ing vi - gil till the morn - ing new
Saw the
C
C6
C7/B♭
F/A
Gm/B♭
F/C
C7
F
77
glo - ry, heard the sto - ry— tid - ings of a gos - pel
F
C/F
F
C
C6
C7/B♭
F/A
Gm/B♭
F/C
C7

80
true. Thus re - joic - ing, free from sor - row, prais - es
F
F
A
B♭2
B♭
Gm
C2
C
Am
83
voic - ing greet the mor - row: Christ, the Babe, was born for
Dm2
Dm
B♭
D
C2
E
C
E
C7
C7
B♭
F
A
Gm
B♭
F
C
C♯°7
86
rit.
(6)
you. Christ, the Babe, was born for you.
Dm
Am
C
C7
B♭
F
A
Gm
B♭
F
C
C7
F
(6)
rit.

He Is Emmanuel

Words and Music by
TRACEY BARKER
Arr. by Steve W. Mauldin

8
is our Lord,
Al - le - lu - ia, do the
A♭ B♭7 E♭
E♭/G
10
an - gels sing,
Al - le - lu - ia to the
A♭ B♭7 E♭
E♭/G
12
King of kings!
mp
Al - le - lu - ia, a
mp
A♭ B♭7 E♭
E♭
E♭/G
mp

14
Child is born,
Al - le - lu - ia, He
A♭ B♭7 E♭
E♭/G
16
is our Lord,
Al - le - lu - ia, do the
A♭ B♭7 E♭
E♭/G
CD: 23
CD: 69
18
an - gels sing,
Al - le - lu - ia to the
A♭ B♭7 E♭
E♭/G

20
mf
King of kings! Glo - ri - a in ex -
mf
A♭ B♭7 E♭ B♭ B♭/D
mf
22
cel - sis De - o! Glo - ri - a to the
A♭/E♭ E♭ Fm/E♭ E♭ Cm B♭ B♭/D
24
Lamb of Is - ra - el! Glo - ri - a in ex -
A♭/E♭ E♭ E♭/G B♭ B♭/D

26

cel - sis De - o! Glo - ri - a, He is Em - man - u - el!

Ab/C Cm7 Fm/C Cm7 Fm/C Cm7 Db

28

Glo - ri - a in ex -

Eb Eb/G Bb Bb/D

30

cel - sis De - o! Glo - ri - a to the

Ab/Eb Eb Fm/Eb Eb Cm Bb Bb/D

32
Lamb of Is - ra - el! Glo - ri - a in ex -
A♭/E♭
E♭
E♭/G
B♭
B♭/D
34
cel - sis De - o! Glo - ri - a,
He is Em - man - u - el!
A♭/C
C m7
F m/C
C m7
F m/C
C m7
D♭
36
CD: 24
CD: 70
E♭
E♭/G
A♭
A♭m/F
E♭/G
A♭m6
E♭/B♭
B♭7
E♭

39
mp
Al - le - lu - ia, such a ti - ny boy,
mp
E♭
E♭/G
A♭ B♭7 E♭
mp
41
Al - le - lu - ia, to bring such joy,
E♭
E♭/G
A♭ B♭7 E♭
43
Al - le - lu - ia, hear the an - thems ring,
E♭
E♭/G
A♭ B♭7 E♭

45
mf
Al - le - lu - ia to the King of kings! Glo - ri -
mf
E♭
E♭/G
A♭
B♭7
E♭
47
a in ex - cel - sis De - o! Glo - ri -
B♭
B♭/D
A♭/E♭
E♭
Fm/E♭
E♭
Cm
mf
49
a to the Lamb of Is - ra - el! Glo - ri -
B♭
B♭/D
A♭/E♭
E♭
E♭/G

51
a in ex - cel - sis De - o! Glo - ri - a,
B♭ B♭/D A♭/C Cm7 Fm/C Cm7 Fm/C Cm7
CD: 25
CD: 71
53
He is Em-man - u - el!
Glo-ri -
f
D♭ E♭ C/E F/A
56
a in ex - cel - sis De - o! Glo - ri -
C C/E B♭/F F Gm/F F Dm
f

58
a to the Lamb of Is - ra - el! Glo - ri -
C C/E B♭/F F F/A
60
a in ex - cel - sis De - o! Glo - ri - a,
C C/E B♭/D Dm7 Gm/D Dm7 Gm/D Dm7
62
He is Em - man - u - el! Glo - ri - a,
E♭ F Dm7

(Without music)

NARRATOR: "He was in the world, and though the world was made through him, the world did not recognize him. He came to that which was his own, but his own did not receive him. *(Very warm and emotional)* Yet to all who received him, to those who believed in his name, he gave the right to become children of God." *(John 1:10)*

(Music begins)

Son of God, Son of Man

15
CD: 27
CD: 73
rit.
way, Long a - go we heard the proph - ets say.
Add MEN mp
Let
B♭2/D
B♭/D
B♭m6/D♭
C sus
C
rit.
18
a tempo
all God's an - gels wor - ship Him, Son of God,
F
C/E
C/G
F
D m
B♭
F/A
B♭2
a tempo
21
Son of Man; O God Your reign will nev - er end,
C sus
C
D m7
B♭/C
F/C
F/B♭
B♭2

CD: 28
CD: 74
rit.
a tempo
Je - sus Son of God, Son of Man.
F/A B♭2 Csus C F C/E C/G F C/E B♭/D B♭
MEN unis. mp
What a like - ness, what a
wonder, That my Lord is, now my broth - er; I can
F2 F B♭2

Add LADIES
34
p
Oo,
reach His hand and see His face, I will
E♭6 9
B♭2/D
B♭/D
CD: 29
36 CD: 75
rit.
mp
a tempo
Oo.
lift my eyes and sing His praise.
Let all God's an - gels
B♭m6/D♭
C sus
C
F
C/F
B♭/F
F
rit.
a tempo
39
wor - ship Him, Son of God, Son of Man; O
Dm
B♭
F/A
B♭2
C sus
C

CD: 30
CD: 76
42
God Your reign will nev - er end, Je - sus Son of
Dm7
B♭/C
F/C
F/B♭
F/A
B♭2
45
mf
God. For now, a lit - tle low - er than the
mf
Csus
C
F/A
B♭
mf
48
f
an - gels, Wear a crown of
f
Fsus
F
D♭
E♭/D♭
cresc.
f

CD: 31
CD: 77
51
glo - ry through the a - ges.
D♭
D♭6
D♭7
54
rit.
a tempo
Let all God's an - gels wor - ship Him,
C M7
D
G
D
F♯
D
A
G
Em
C2
rit.
a tempo
57
Son of God, Son of Man; O God Your reign will
G
B
C2
Dsus
D
Em7
C
D
G
D

CD: 32

CD: 78

60

ff

nev - er end, Je - sus Son of God. Let

G/C C2 G/B C2 Dsus D E♭/D♭

dim.

63

all God's an - gels wor - ship Him, Son of God,

A♭ E♭/G E♭/B♭ A♭ Fm D♭2 A♭/C D♭2

ff

66

dim.

Son of Man; O God Your reign will nev - er end,

E♭sus E♭ Fm7 D♭/E♭ A♭/E♭ A♭/D♭ D♭2

dim.

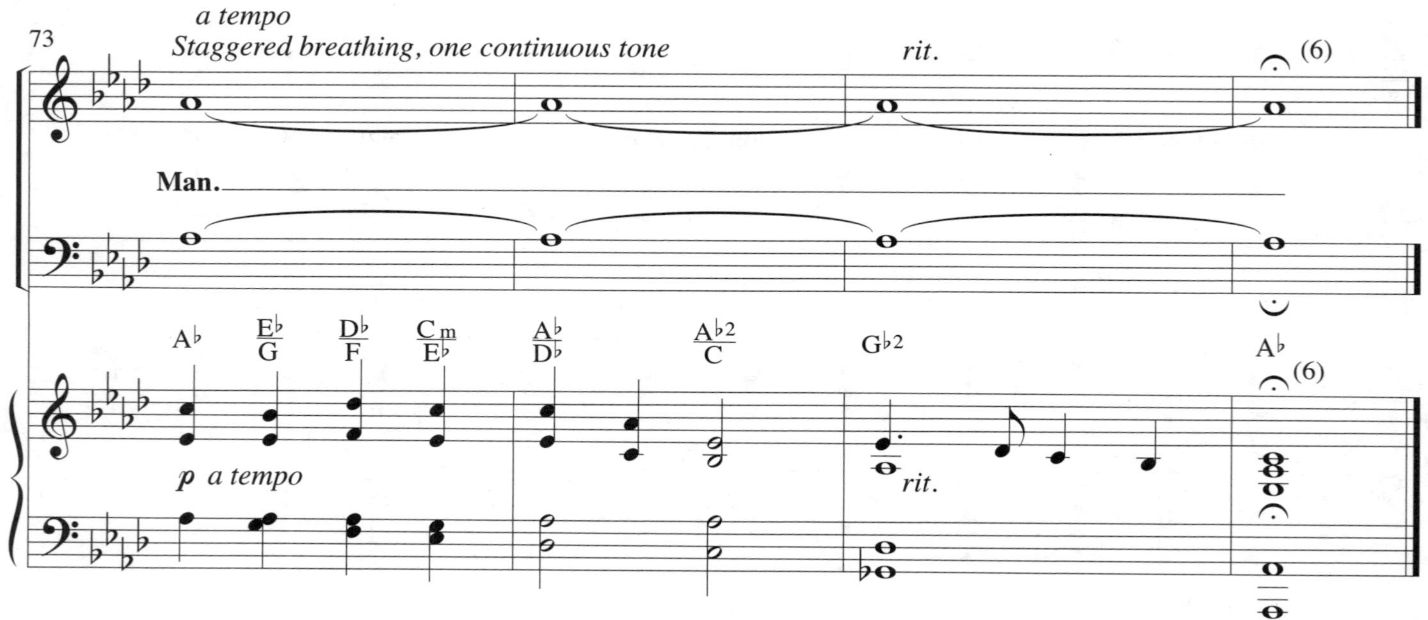

(Without music)

NARRATOR: John, chapter 8, verse 12, records the words of Jesus when he said, "I am the light of the world. Whoever follows me will never walk in darkness, *(upbeat and energetic)* but will have the light of life."

(Music begins)

Every Light That Shines at Christmas

Words and Music by
WAYNE HAUN, JOEL LINDEY and ERNIE HAASE
Arr. by Steve W. Mauldin

13
gift un - der the tree;
Ev - 'ry
C
17
hall that's decked with hol - ly,
ev - 'ry
F
21
car - ol that we sing.
Ev - 'ry
D 7
G
E
G♯

25
wide - eyed kid that's wish - ing for a
Am
F7
29
cold and snow - y morn'; Ev - 'ry
Am
D7
C
E
33
light that shines at Christ - mas shouts, "Hal - le - lu -
F
C
E
F
Gm
E

37
CD: 34
CD: 80
mel.
mel.
- jah! Christ is born!" Ev - 'ry
Gm/E
F
C/G
G
C
41
light that shines at Christ - mas, ev - 'ry
C
45
gift un - der the tree; Ev - 'ry
C

49
hall that's decked with hol - ly, ev - 'ry
F
53
car - ol that we sing. Ev - 'ry
D 7
G
E
G♯
57
wide - eyed kid that's wish - ing for a
A m
F 7

61
cold and snow - y morn'; Ev - 'ry
Am
D7
C/E
65
light that shines at Christ - mas shouts, "Hal - le - lu -
F
C/E
F
Gm/E
69
CD: 35
CD: 81
mel.
- jah! Christ is born!"
Gm/E
F
C/G
G
C

73
Wise men saw a light shin -
C
F
77
- ing in the sky all those man - y years a - go;
C
G
81
They fol - lowed thro' the night with -
C
F

85

out ask - ing why ___ to the ba - by in the swad - dl - ing clothes. ___

C G

89

___

MEN *unis.* So to - day we string up spar - kl - ing lights ___

C F E♭ C

93

___ from our hous - es to the tops of our trees; ___

C F E♭ C

*NOTE: If using a reprise and trax, start at CD point 36 or 82. Vocals start singing at measure 106.

109
- mas,
ev - 'ry gift un - der the tree;
C
113
Ev - 'ry hall that's decked with hol -
C
F
117
- ly,
ev - 'ry car - ol that we sing.
F
D 7

121
Ev - 'ry wide - eyed kid that's wish -
G
E
G♯
Am
125
- ing for a cold and snow - y morn';
F7
Am
129
Ev - 'ry light that shines at Christ -
D7
C
E
F
C
E

133
- mas shouts, "Hal - le - lu - jah! Christ is
C/E
F
Gm/E
F
C/G
G
CD: 37
CD: 83
137
born!"
C
141
ALTOS
MEN unis.
I've got a light!
I've got a light!
G

145
SOPRANOS
LADIES div.
I've got a light!
Let it shine, shine, shine!
TENORS
G
G°7
Am/G
G
149
Let it shine!
BASSES
I'm gon-na let it shine!
G
C
153
CD: 38
CD: 84
Let it shine! Let it shine!
TENORS
C

157
Ev - 'ry light that shines at Christ -
BASSES
I'm gon-na let it shine!
C
N.C.
C
161
- mas, ev - 'ry gift un - der the tree;
C
165
Ev - 'ry hall that's decked with hol -
C
F

169
-ly, ev-'ry car-ol that we sing.
F
D7
173
Ev-'ry wide-eyed kid that's wish-
G
E
G♯
Am
177
-ing for a cold and snow-y morn';
F7
Am

181
Ev - 'ry light that shines at Christ -
D 7
C/E
F
C/E
185
CD: 39
CD: 85
- mas shouts, "Hal - le - lu - jah! Christ is
C/E
F
Gm/E
F
C/G
G
189
born!" Ev - 'ry light that shines at Christ -
C
C/E
F
C/E

193
- mas shouts, "Hal - le - lu - jah!"
C/E
F
Gm/E
F
N.C.
Gm/E
197
Shout, "Hal - le - lu - jah!"
Gm/E
F
N.C.
Gm/E
F
N.C.
Gm/E
201
Shout, "Hal - le - lu - jah!
Gm/E
F
N.C.
Gm/E
F

*NOTE: If using the Reprise and Trax, start at CD point 36 or 82 on page 65.

Come and Adore Him Finale

includes
Come and Adore Him
Angels, from the Realms of Glory

CD: 40 In two ♩. = ca. 58
CD: 86

Arr. by Steve W. Mauldin

N.C. D Em

mf

3 D/F♯ GM7 A E♭

f

6 A♭M7 A♭6 A♭2 Gm7 Fm7 E♭/G B♭sus B♭

9 *"Come and Adore Him"
mf CHOIR *div.*

Come, come and a-dore Him, Fall-ing be-fore Him, Wor-ship the

mf

E♭ Fm7 E♭/G

mf

*Words and Music by REBECCA J. PECK.

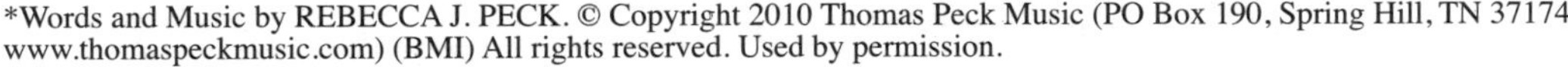

12
Lord of lords; Come in - to His pres - ence, Glo - ry and
A♭M7
B♭
E♭
Fm7
15
rev-'rence, Be to His name ev - er - more. God Him - self,
E♭/G
A♭M7
B♭
G/B
Cm
18
here to dwell a-mong men;
F/A
B♭
A♭2

CD: 41
CD: 87

21

Come, come and a - dore Him.

Fm4 7 Ab/G AbM7 Bbsus Bb Eb

24

There is a place at the man-ger,

AbM7 Bb/Ab Ab Ab/Bb Bb Eb Ebsus

27

Where all who seek Him can kneel; Hon - or - ing this ho - ly

Bb/Eb Eb

30
Sav - ior,
See - ing God's prom - ise re - vealed.
E♭sus
D♭
B♭sus
B♭
33
Bow down in hum - ble a - maze - ment,
Just to be - hold de - i -
Cm
A♭2
E♭/G
A♭2
CD: 42
CD: 88
36
ty;
Join with the shep - herds to praise Him,
B♭sus
B♭
Cm
A♭2

39
Giv - ing your heart to the King.
Come, come and a-dore
E♭/G
A♭2
B♭sus
B♭
F
42
Him, Fall - ing be-fore Him, Wor-ship the Lord of lords;
Gm7
F/A
B♭M7
C
45
Come in - to His pres - ence, Glo - ry and
F
Gm7

47
rev-'rence, Be to His name ev-er-more. God Him-self,
F/A
B♭M7
C
A/C♯
Dm
50
here to dwell a-mong men;
G/B
C
B♭2
CD: 43
CD: 89
53
Come, come and a - dore Him.
Gm4 7
B♭/A
B♭M7
Csus
C
F

56
LADIES unis.
There is a mo - ment of won - der,
Fm
Gm/F
Fm7
B♭
A♭/B♭
B♭
E♭
E♭sus
59
For those who look on His face;
Find - ing a joy like no
B♭/E♭
E♭
62
oth - er,
Wrapped up in rags on the hay.
E♭sus
D♭
B♭sus
B♭
(♮)

65
He who is from ev - er - last - ing,
Left heav - en's throne a -
Add MEN
Cm
A♭2
E♭/G
A♭2
68
CD: 44
CD: 90
bove;
Lift up an an - them of bless - ing,
B♭sus
B♭
Cm
A♭2
71
For this un - speak - a - ble love.
f
Come, come and a - dore
E♭/G
A♭2
B♭sus
B♭
F

74
Him, Fall-ing be-fore Him, Wor-ship the Lord of lords;
Gm7
F/A
B♭M7
C
77
Come in-to His pres-ence, Glo-ry and
F
Gm7
79
rev-'rence, Be to His name ev-er-more. God Him-self,
F/A
B♭M7
C
A/C♯
Dm

*Words by JAMES MONTGOMERY; Music by HENRY T. SMART. Arr.

90
Come and wor - ship. Wor - ship Christ, the new - born King.
B
B
D♯
Em
Am
G
B
Am
C
C
E
Dsus
D
G
93
Come and wor - ship. Come and wor - ship. Wor - ship Christ, the
D
D
C
B
B
D♯
Em
Am
G
B
Am
C
C
E
CD: 46
CD: 92
Like beginning ♩. = ca. 58
96
new - born King.
G
D
D
G

99

Come and wor - ship. Come and wor - ship.

G N.C. D D/C B B/D♯ Em

102

Wor - ship Christ, the new - born King. Come and wor - ship.

Am G/B Am/C Em Dsus D G D D/C

105

cresc.

Come and wor - ship. Wor - ship Christ, the new -

cresc.

B B/D♯ Em Am G/B Am/C Em G/D

cresc.

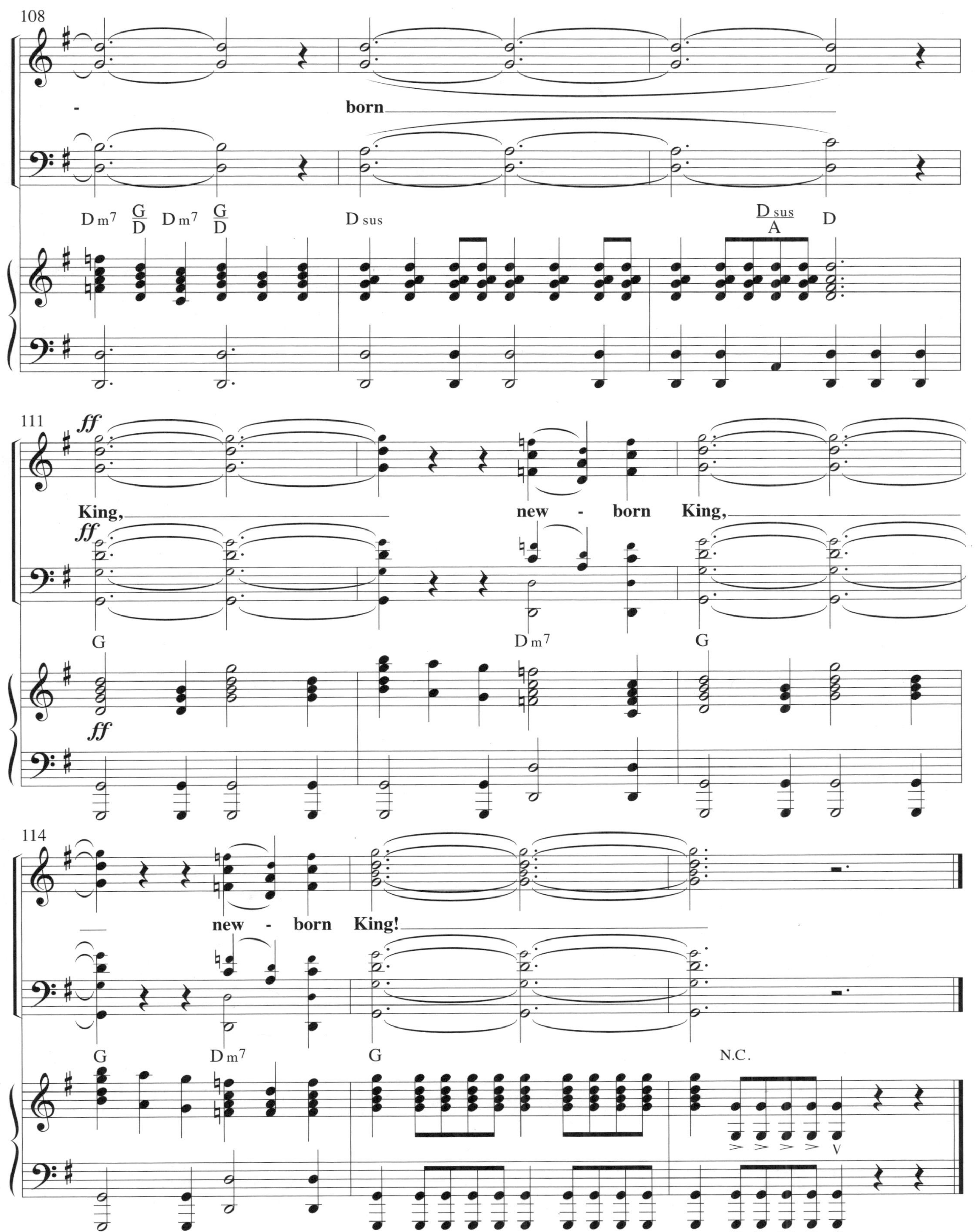
108
born
Dm7
G/D
Dm7
G/D
Dsus
Dsus/A
D
111
ff
King,
new - born King,
ff
G
Dm7
G
ff
114
new - born King!
G
Dm7
G
N.C.